Cologne Tra
2024

CW01455690

Cologne Unveiled: A Comprehensive Travel Guide for an Enriching Journey in 2024

MICKEY ALLEN

© 2024 Mickey Allen all rights reserved.

No part of this travel guide may be reproduced, distributed, or transmitted in any form or by any means, including photocopying, recording, or other electronic or mechanical methods, without the prior written permission of the publisher, except in the case of brief quotations embodied in critical reviews and certain other noncommercial uses permitted by copyright law.

Contents

Chapter 1: Introduction to Cologne

Overview of Cologne's Geography, History, and Significance

Cologne, situated along the banks of the Rhine River in western Germany, is a city rich in history, culture, and architectural marvels.

Geography: Cologne boasts a strategic location, serving as a major European transportation hub. Its position on the Rhine River has played a crucial role in its development as a cultural and economic center. The city is characterized by a blend of modernity and historical charm, with the towering spires of its iconic cathedral dominating the skyline.

History: Tracing its roots back to Roman times, Cologne has a fascinating history that unfolds through its well-preserved landmarks. The city's ancient Roman walls and gates stand testament to its role as a significant Roman provincial capital, known as Colonia Claudia Ara Agrippinensium. Over the centuries, Cologne has evolved into a thriving metropolis, overcoming the challenges of war and rebuilding itself into a vibrant cultural hub.

Significance: Cologne holds a special place in Germany's cultural tapestry. Home to the renowned Cologne Cathedral (Kölner Dom), a UNESCO World Heritage site, the city attracts millions of visitors each year. The cathedral, with its Gothic architecture, is not only a religious symbol but also a representation of Cologne's resilience and architectural prowess. Beyond its religious significance, Cologne is a cultural melting pot, embracing diversity and offering a unique blend of tradition and modernity.

As you embark on your journey through Cologne, the intertwining threads of its geography, history, and significance will unravel, allowing you to immerse yourself in a city that seamlessly connects the past with the present. This vibrant metropolis is ready to captivate you with its stories and landmarks, promising an unforgettable travel experience in 2024.

Brief Introduction to Cologne's Culture and Traditions

Cologne's vibrant culture is a captivating tapestry woven from a rich history, diverse influences, and a strong sense of community. As you explore the city, you'll discover that Cologne's culture is as warm and welcoming as its people.

Festivals and Celebrations: Cologne is renowned for its lively festivals that celebrate both tradition and modernity. The Cologne Carnival, held in the weeks leading up to Lent, is a spectacular event filled with parades, costumes, and exuberant celebrations. The city comes alive with music, dance, and the unmistakable aroma of traditional carnival treats, providing visitors with a unique glimpse into the heart of Cologne's joyous spirit.

Art and Music: Artistic expression thrives in Cologne, with numerous galleries, theaters, and live music venues scattered throughout the city. The city's commitment to the arts is evident in its support for local artists and the vibrant street art scene. Cologne's love for music is deeply ingrained, and you can experience everything from classical performances at the Philharmonic Hall to the pulsating beats of electronic music in trendy clubs.

Culinary Traditions: Cologne's culinary scene reflects its diverse cultural influences. Traditional dishes, such as the hearty "Himmel un Ääd" (Heaven and Earth) or the iconic "Halve Hahn" sandwich, provide a taste of local flavors. Exploring the city's breweries, you'll encounter the famous Kölsch beer, an integral part of Cologne's social fabric. Embrace the local tradition of "Kölsche Etiquette" as you savor these culinary delights.

Community Spirit: Cologne's friendly and open-minded residents contribute to a strong sense of community. Locals, known for their "Kölsche Hätz" (Cologne heart), are more than willing to share stories, recommend hidden gems, and make visitors feel at home. Embrace the opportunity to interact with the people, participate in local events, and gain a deeper understanding of Cologne's unique cultural identity.

In this diverse and dynamic city, culture and tradition intertwine, creating an atmosphere that is both contemporary and deeply rooted in history. As you embark on your journey through Cologne, immerse yourself in the city's cultural tapestry, and let the warmth of its traditions leave a lasting impression on your travel experience in 2024.

Chapter 2: Planning Your Trip

Best Time to Visit Cologne

Choosing the ideal time to visit Cologne ensures that you experience the city at its most vibrant and enjoyable. Each season in Cologne offers a unique charm, allowing you to tailor your visit to your preferred weather and activities.

Spring (March to May): Spring marks the awakening of Cologne's lush greenery and colorful blooms. The weather becomes milder, making it an excellent time for outdoor exploration. The city's parks and gardens, such as the idyllic Rheinpark, come to life, offering a picturesque backdrop for leisurely strolls along the Rhine River.

Summer (June to August): Summer in Cologne brings a lively atmosphere and a calendar filled with outdoor events and festivals. The warm temperatures invite visitors to enjoy al fresco dining in the city's beer gardens, explore outdoor markets, and attend open-air concerts. The longer days provide ample time to discover Cologne's landmarks and take advantage of various recreational activities.

Autumn (September to November): As the summer crowds disperse, autumn unveils a quieter, more contemplative side of Cologne. The weather remains pleasant, and the changing foliage adds a touch of warmth to the city's landscapes. Autumn is an ideal time for cultural pursuits, such as exploring museums, attending art exhibitions, and enjoying the city's diverse culinary scene.

Winter (December to February): Cologne transforms into a winter wonderland during the holiday season. The Christmas markets, with their festive decorations and aromatic treats, create a magical ambiance. While winter temperatures can be cooler, the charm of the city's architecture, illuminated by holiday lights, makes it a captivating time to visit. Don't miss the chance to experience the Cologne Cathedral against the backdrop of a winter skyline.

Special Events: Consider aligning your visit with one of Cologne's signature events, such as the Cologne

Carnival in February or the Summerjam Festival in July. These festivities provide an immersive experience into the city's culture and traditions.

Ultimately, the best time to visit Cologne depends on your preferences and the experiences you seek. Whether you prefer the blooming colors of spring, the festive spirit of winter, or anything in between, Cologne awaits with open arms, ready to offer a memorable experience in 2024.

Visa Requirements and Travel Essentials

Before embarking on your journey to Cologne, it's essential to ensure that you have all the necessary documents and information to make your visit smooth and hassle-free.

Visa Requirements: Check whether you need a visa to enter Germany and, consequently, Cologne. Visitors from many countries, including those in the European Union and the United States, typically do not need a visa for short stays. However, it's crucial to confirm the specific requirements based on your nationality and the purpose of your visit. Visit the official German embassy or consulate website to obtain up-to-date information on visa regulations and the application process.

Passport: Ensure that your passport is valid for at least six months beyond your planned departure date. Check for any visa stamps or entry requirements, and make photocopies of important pages, such as the main identification page and any relevant visa pages, to keep in a separate, secure location.

Travel Insurance: Consider obtaining travel insurance that covers medical emergencies, trip cancellations, and other unforeseen events. This provides peace of mind and financial protection in case of unexpected circumstances during your travels.

Health Precautions: Check if any vaccinations are required before traveling to Cologne. Carry any necessary medications and a basic first aid kit. Familiarize yourself with local medical facilities and emergency contact numbers.

Currency and Banking: The official currency in Germany is the Euro (€). Inform your bank about your travel dates to avoid any issues with using your credit or debit cards abroad. ATMs are widely available in Cologne, providing convenient access to cash.

Communication: While English is widely spoken, it's helpful to learn a few basic German phrases. Ensure your mobile phone is unlocked for international use or consider purchasing a local SIM card for communication during your stay.

Transportation: Research and plan your transportation within Cologne. The city has an efficient public transportation system, including buses, trams, and the U-Bahn (subway). Familiarize yourself with ticket options and schedules to navigate the city conveniently.

By taking care of these essential travel requirements, you'll set the foundation for a smooth and enjoyable visit to Cologne. Planning ahead ensures that you can focus on experiencing the city's attractions, culture, and cuisine with peace of mind in 2024.

Transportation Options and Getting Around

Navigating the charming streets of Cologne is a delightful part of the travel experience. The city offers a well-connected and efficient transportation system that allows visitors to explore its diverse neighborhoods and iconic landmarks seamlessly.

Public Transportation: Cologne's public transportation system is a convenient way to traverse the city. The extensive network includes buses, trams, and the U-Bahn (subway). Tickets can be purchased at stations or on board, and various options, including day passes, offer flexibility for exploring different parts of the city. Keep in mind that Cologne's compact city center is easily walkable, allowing you to discover many attractions on foot.

Biking: Cologne is a bicycle-friendly city with dedicated bike lanes and rental services available. Exploring the city on two wheels provides a unique perspective, allowing you to meander along the Rhine River or visit parks and attractions with ease. Several bike rental companies operate in the city, offering a convenient and eco-friendly way to get around.

Taxi and Ride-Sharing Services: Taxis are readily available in Cologne and can be found at designated taxi stands or hailed on the street. Additionally, ride-sharing services provide a modern and accessible alternative for getting around the city. Make sure to check the official taxi rates and use reputable ride-sharing apps for a reliable and safe experience.

Car Rentals: While public transportation is efficient, renting a car can be advantageous if you plan to explore the surrounding regions or venture into the picturesque German countryside. Rental agencies are located throughout the city, and driving in Cologne is generally straightforward. However, be mindful of parking regulations and the availability of parking spaces in the city center.

Rhine River Cruises: For a unique and scenic perspective of Cologne, consider taking a Rhine River cruise. These leisurely boat rides offer panoramic views of the city's skyline, including iconic landmarks like the Cologne Cathedral. Cruises vary in duration, providing an enjoyable and relaxing way to experience the city from the water.

Cologne's diverse transportation options cater to various preferences, ensuring that you can explore the city comfortably and efficiently. Whether you choose to stroll through historic streets, cycle along the riverbanks, or utilize the well-connected public transportation, each mode of transport adds its own charm to your travel experience in 2024.

Must-Visit Landmarks and Historical Sites

Cologne is a city steeped in history, and its skyline is adorned with iconic landmarks that tell tales of centuries gone by. As you embark on your exploration of this captivating city, be sure to include these must-visit landmarks and historical sites in your itinerary:

1. **Cologne Cathedral (Kölner Dom):**

   - Dominating the city's skyline, the Cologne Cathedral is an architectural masterpiece and a UNESCO World Heritage site. Its Gothic spires and intricate details draw millions of visitors each year. Take the time to explore the interior, marvel at the panoramic views from the tower, and appreciate the spiritual and historical significance of this imposing structure.

Rheinpark at the back

2. Hohenzollern Bridge (Hohenzollernbrücke):

- Stretching across the Rhine River, the Hohenzollern Bridge is not only a vital transportation link but also a symbol of love and commitment. Thousands of love locks attached to the bridge's railings create a unique and romantic atmosphere. Enjoy a leisurely stroll across the bridge and capture breathtaking views of the city.

3. Cologne Old Town (Altstadt):

- Wander through the narrow cobblestone streets of the Old Town, where historic buildings and charming squares transport you back in time. Explore the Alter Markt, home to the City Hall (Rathaus) and the Jan von Werth Fountain. Be sure to visit the Great St. Martin Church, a Romanesque gem nestled in the heart of the Old Town.

4. **Roman-Germanic Museum (Römisch-Germanisches Museum):**

- Uncover the city's Roman roots at the Roman-Germanic Museum. Housing an extensive collection of artifacts, including the famous Dionysus mosaic, the museum provides a fascinating glimpse into Cologne's past as a Roman provincial capital.

5. **Farina Fragrance Museum (Farina-Haus):**

- Step into the world of fragrance at the Farina Fragrance Museum, where the world's first Eau de Cologne was created. Discover the history of perfume production and explore the elegant rooms of the museum, which transport you to the 18th century.

6. **Ludwig Museum (Ludwig Museum):**

- Art enthusiasts will appreciate the Ludwig Museum, showcasing a remarkable collection of modern and contemporary art. From Pop Art to Abstract Expressionism, the museum provides a diverse and thought-provoking artistic experience.

7. **Kolumba Art Museum (Kolumba Kunstmuseum):**

- Located on the site of the former St. Kolumba Church, the Kolumba Art Museum seamlessly blends the old with the new. This architectural gem houses a collection of religious art, offering a serene and contemplative space for visitors.

These landmarks and historical sites are just a glimpse into the rich tapestry of Cologne's history and cultural heritage. Each visit unfolds new stories, allowing you to appreciate the city's legacy and architectural wonders in 2024.

Natural Wonders and Scenic Spots

While Cologne is renowned for its historical landmarks, the city also boasts natural wonders and scenic spots that showcase its diverse landscapes and provide moments of tranquility amid urban life. Explore these delightful locations to experience the beauty of Cologne's natural surroundings:

1. **Rheinpark:**

   - Nestled along the banks of the Rhine River, Rheinpark is a sprawling green oasis offering breathtaking views of the water and the city skyline. Stroll along the promenade, relax on the lawns, or enjoy a picnic with the iconic Cologne Cathedral as your backdrop.

2. **Flora and Botanical Garden (Flora und Botanischer Garten Köln):**

   - Immerse yourself in the beauty of nature at the Flora and Botanical Garden. This botanical paradise showcases a wide variety of plant species in themed gardens, providing a serene escape from the bustling city. Explore the tropical greenhouses and discover the seasonal floral displays.

3. **Aachener Weiher:**

- Aachener Weiher is a picturesque lake surrounded by lush greenery, located in the heart of the city's university district. It's a popular spot for locals and visitors alike, offering a peaceful retreat for a leisurely stroll, a boat ride, or simply enjoying the serenity by the water.

4. **Decksteiner Weiher:**

- For those seeking a more secluded natural escape, Decksteiner Weiher is a tranquil lake surrounded by woodlands. The walking trails around the lake provide a serene environment for nature enthusiasts, birdwatchers, and those looking for a peaceful retreat.

5. **Poller Wiesen:**

   - This expansive riverside meadow, known as Poller Wiesen, is an ideal spot for outdoor activities and relaxation. With the Rhine on one side and the cityscape on the other, it's a popular destination for locals to unwind, have a barbecue, or engage in recreational sports.

6. **Eigelsteintorburg Gardens (Gärten des Eigelsteintores):**

   - Tucked away behind the historic Eigelsteintorburg gate, these gardens offer a charming blend of greenery and historical architecture. The peaceful setting invites visitors to enjoy a quiet moment surrounded by flowers, sculptures, and the remnants of the old city walls.

7. **Klettenbergpark:**

   - Klettenbergpark is a serene urban park that provides a peaceful escape from the city's hustle and bustle. With its tree-lined paths, open spaces, and a pond, it's a favorite spot for locals to unwind and enjoy nature.

Discovering these natural wonders and scenic spots allows you to experience the harmonious balance between urban life and nature that defines Cologne. Take the time to rejuvenate your spirit amidst these picturesque settings in 2024.

Hidden Gems and Off-the-Beaten-Path Discoveries

Cologne's charm extends beyond its well-known landmarks, revealing hidden gems and off-the-beaten-path treasures waiting to be discovered. Venture off the tourist track to uncover the city's unique and lesser-known attractions that add an extra layer of enchantment to your visit:

1. **Melaten Cemetery (Melatenfriedhof):**

   - This historic cemetery, with its tree-lined avenues and artistic tombstones, is a peaceful and contemplative space. Melaten Cemetery is not only a resting place for many notable figures but also a serene oasis for a quiet stroll amid nature and history.

2. **St. Gereon's Basilica (Basilika St. Gereon):**

- Often overshadowed by the Cologne Cathedral, St. Gereon's Basilica is a hidden gem of Romanesque architecture. The basilica's unique design and ancient history make it a fascinating and lesser-explored site.

3. **Lindenthaler Tierpark:**

- Escape the urban hustle with a visit to Lindenthaler Tierpark, Cologne's charming zoo. While smaller than some larger zoos, it offers a more intimate experience and houses a variety of animals in a serene setting.

4. **St. Aposteln Church (Basilika St. Aposteln):**

   - Step into the quiet elegance of St. Aposteln Church, a Romanesque gem that often escapes the tourist radar. Admire its medieval architecture, beautiful stained glass windows, and the tranquil atmosphere within.

5. **Kolumba Archaeological Zone (Kolumba Archäologische Zone):**

   - Beneath the Kolumba Art Museum lies an archaeological site revealing layers of Cologne's history. Explore the remains of Roman buildings and medieval structures, providing a fascinating glimpse into the city's past.

6. **Eigelsteintorburg:**

   - This historic gate, Eigelsteintorburg, is a well-preserved relic from Cologne's medieval fortifications. Hidden within the city, it offers a glimpse into the architectural history of the area, with its towers and defensive structures.

7. **Gross St. Martin:**

- While not entirely hidden, Gross St. Martin is often overshadowed by the Cologne Cathedral. This Romanesque church along the Rhine River features a unique three-towered facade and a peaceful courtyard, providing a quiet retreat in the heart of the city.

8. **Agnesviertel:**

- Explore the eclectic and artistic neighborhood of Agnesviertel. Filled with colorful facades, trendy boutiques, and cozy cafes, this area provides a different perspective of Cologne's vibrant culture away from the mainstream.

Embrace the spirit of exploration and seek out these hidden gems to uncover the lesser-known stories and facets of Cologne.

Chapter 4: Culinary Delights of Cologne

Introduction to Cologne Cuisine

Cologne's culinary scene is a delectable fusion of traditional German flavors, regional specialties, and a dash of international influence. As you embark on a culinary journey through the city, prepare your taste buds for a delightful exploration of Cologne cuisine:

1. **Kölsch Beer:**

   - Begin your culinary adventure with a sip of Kölsch, the local beer that holds a special place in the hearts of Cologne's residents. Served in small, slender glasses, this pale, top-fermented beer is not just a beverage but a cultural experience. Enjoy it in one of the city's historic breweries, where the distinctive Kölsch etiquette adds a sociable touch to your drink.

2. Himmel un Ääd (Heaven and Earth):

- A classic dish of Cologne, Himmel un Ääd is a hearty combination of mashed potatoes (representing "earth") and apple sauce (representing "heaven"). Often accompanied by black pudding or slices of blood sausage, this dish reflects the region's agricultural roots and offers a satisfying blend of sweet and savory flavors.

3. Halve Hahn:

- Despite its name, Halve Hahn is not a chicken dish but rather a rye bread roll with Gouda cheese, mustard, and onions. This simple and beloved snack is a popular choice in Cologne's pubs and beer gardens, providing a tasty and uncomplicated treat for locals and visitors alike.

4. **Rheinischer Sauerbraten:**

   - This traditional pot roast, marinated in a sour and sweet broth, is a culinary gem hailing from the Rhineland region. Typically served with red cabbage and potato dumplings, Rheinischer Sauerbraten showcases the Germans' mastery of transforming humble ingredients into a flavorful feast.

5. **Reibekuchen:**

   - Enjoy a comforting plate of Reibekuchen, crispy potato pancakes often served with applesauce. Whether enjoyed as a snack at a Christmas market or as a side dish in a cozy tavern, these golden delights are a delightful representation of Cologne's winter culinary traditions.

6. **Cologne Mustard (Kölscher Senf):**

   - Elevate your meals with a dollop of Cologne Mustard, known for its spiciness and unique flavor profile. Whether paired with sausages, pretzels, or meats, this local condiment adds a zesty kick to your culinary adventures.

7. **Schnitzel:**

- While Schnitzel is not exclusive to Cologne, the city's variations offer a local twist. Try a Cologne-style Schnitzel, where the breaded and fried meat is often served with a caper and anchovy sauce, providing a delightful contrast of flavors.

Cologne cuisine is a celebration of hearty, flavorsome dishes that reflect the region's history and cultural influences. From the lively atmosphere of beer gardens to the cozy warmth of traditional taverns, immerse yourself in the culinary tapestry of Cologne in 2024.

Popular Local Dishes and Where to Try Them

Embark on a gastronomic journey through Cologne and savor the city's signature dishes at these popular establishments that have become culinary landmarks in their own right:

1. **Früh am Dom:**

   - **Signature Dish:** Kölsch Beer

   - **Where to Try It:** Früh am Dom, one of Cologne's most iconic breweries located near the cathedral. Enjoy the convivial atmosphere as you savor the locally brewed Kölsch, served with a side of traditional pub fare. The lively ambiance and historic setting make this an ideal spot to experience the Kölsch culture.

2. **Peters Brauhaus:**

   - **Signature Dish:** Himmel un Ääd

   - **Where to Try It:** Peters Brauhaus, a historic brewery with a warm and rustic charm. Indulge in the classic Cologne dish, Himmel un Ääd, amidst the brewery's traditional setting. The combination of mashed potatoes and apple sauce, paired with the unique character of Peters Brauhaus, creates a memorable dining experience.

3. **Gilden im Zims:**

   - **Signature Dish:** Halve Hahn

   - **Where to Try It:** Gilden im Zims, a cozy tavern in the heart of the Old Town. Delight in the simplicity of Halve Hahn – a rye bread roll with Gouda cheese, mustard, and onions – in this charming establishment. The historic surroundings and local atmosphere make it an ideal place to sample this Cologne classic.

4. **Em Golde Kappes:**

   - **Signature Dish:** Rheinischer Sauerbraten

   - **Where to Try It:** Em Golde Kappes, a traditional Cologne restaurant known for its authentic regional cuisine. Experience the rich flavors of Rheinischer Sauerbraten, a pot roast marinated in a sour and sweet broth, in the welcoming ambiance of this local favorite.

5. **Päffgen:**

- **Signature Dish:** Reibekuchen

- **Where to Try It:** Päffgen, a historic brewhouse dating back to 1883. Indulge in the crispy delight of Reibekuchen, potato pancakes often enjoyed with applesauce, in the rustic surroundings of Päffgen. The combination of traditional flavors and a lively atmosphere makes this brewery a must-visit for culinary enthusiasts.

6. **Lommerzheim:**

- **Signature Dish:** Cologne Mustard (Kölscher Senf)

- **Where to Try It:** Lommerzheim, a legendary tavern renowned for its local atmosphere. Enhance your meals with the distinctive spiciness of Cologne Mustard, served alongside a variety of dishes in this traditional setting. The hearty pub fare and welcoming ambiance make Lommerzheim a favorite among locals.

7. **Eigelsteintorburg:**

- **Signature Dish:** Schnitzel

- **Where to Try It:** Eigelsteintorburg, a historic gate turned restaurant. Relish the Cologne-style Schnitzel, breaded and fried to perfection, in the unique ambiance of Eigelsteintorburg. The caper and anchovy sauce add a local twist to this classic dish, making it a delightful culinary experience.

Venture into these renowned establishments to not only savor the authentic flavors of Cologne but also immerse yourself in the local culture and traditions that define each dining experience in 2024.

Dining Etiquette and Recommended Restaurants

Indulging in Cologne's culinary scene extends beyond the flavors on your plate; it's an immersive experience influenced by local customs and hospitality. Familiarize yourself with dining etiquette and explore these recommended restaurants for an authentic taste of Cologne:

Dining Etiquette:

1. **Reservations:** While not always mandatory, making reservations, especially for dinner in popular restaurants, is advisable to secure your spot.

2. **Tipping:** Tipping is customary in Cologne. A service charge is often included in the bill, but it's common to round up the total or leave a small additional tip for good service.

3. **Paying the Bill:** In restaurants, it's customary for the waiter to bring the bill to your table. You can pay directly at your table or at the cash register, depending on the establishment.

4. **Kölsch Etiquette:** When enjoying Kölsch beer, a waiter will continuously bring you refills unless you signal to stop by placing a beer mat on top of your empty glass. Keep track of the number of refills, as this will determine your final bill.

Recommended Restaurants:

1. **Schreckenskammer:**

   - *Location:* Ubierring 13, 50678 Köln, Germany

   - *Description:* Schreckenskammer offers a cozy atmosphere with a menu featuring a mix of regional and international dishes. Known for its creative culinary twists, it's a great choice for those seeking a modern take on traditional Cologne cuisine.

2. **Zum Scheuen Reh:**

   - *Location:* Eigelstein 74, 50668 Köln, Germany

   - *Description:* Nestled in the lively Eigelstein district, Zum Scheuen Reh is a traditional tavern that captures the essence of Cologne. With a menu showcasing local specialties, it's an ideal spot to immerse yourself in the city's culinary traditions.

3. **Lommerzheim:**

- *Location:* Siegesstraße 18, 50679 Köln, Germany

- *Description:* Lommerzheim, a legendary tavern, is celebrated for its hearty Cologne cuisine and welcoming ambiance. Frequented by locals, it provides an authentic experience, and its traditional pub fare is a testament to the city's culinary heritage.

4. **Oma Kleinmann's:**

- *Location:* Zülpicher Str. 9, 50674 Köln, Germany

- *Description:* Oma Kleinmann's is a charming restaurant famous for its generous portions and homey atmosphere. Specializing in hearty German dishes, it's a favorite among both locals and visitors seeking an authentic dining experience.

5. **Bei Oma Kleinmann:**

- *Location:* Severinstraße 56, 50678 Köln, Germany

- *Description:* Bei Oma Kleinmann, located in the Südstadt district, is renowned for its cozy setting and traditional Cologne dishes. The friendly ambiance and flavorful cuisine make it a beloved spot for those seeking an authentic taste of the city.

Cologne's dining scene offers a delightful blend of tradition and innovation. Whether you choose a historic tavern or a modern restaurant, each establishment contributes to the vibrant culinary tapestry of the city, ensuring a memorable dining experience in 2024.

Chapter 5: Outdoor Adventures

Hiking Trails and Trekking Routes

Cologne may be known for its urban allure, but nature enthusiasts will find solace in the picturesque hiking trails and trekking routes that surround the city. Lace up your hiking boots and explore the scenic landscapes just a stone's throw away from the vibrant streets of Cologne:

1. **Kölnpfad (Cologne Trail):**

   - *Description:* The Kölnpfad offers a diverse hiking experience, winding through the outskirts of Cologne and providing stunning views of the city and its surroundings. The trail encompasses a mix of woodlands, meadows, and panoramic viewpoints. Choose from different sections to tailor your hike to your preferred distance and difficulty level.

2. **Wahner Heide Nature Reserve:**

   - *Description:* Located southeast of Cologne, the Wahner Heide Nature Reserve is a vast area of heathland and woods, offering an immersive natural experience. Hiking trails meander through the heath, providing opportunities for birdwatching and peaceful strolls. The reserve's varied landscapes make it an ideal destination for nature enthusiasts.

3. **Rodenkirchener Rheinuferweg:**

   - *Description:* The Rodenkirchener Rheinuferweg is a scenic trail along the Rhine River in the southern part of Cologne. Perfect for a leisurely walk or a longer trek, the trail offers river views, green meadows, and the chance to discover charming villages along the way.

4. **Dünnwalder Wald:**

- *Description:* The Dünnwalder Wald, or Dünnwald Forest, is a serene wooded area northeast of Cologne. Explore its network of trails, surrounded by lush greenery and tranquility. The forest provides a peaceful escape, and the well-maintained paths cater to both casual strollers and avid hikers.

5. **Bergisches Land:**

- *Description:* For a more challenging trek, venture into the Bergisches Land region, located east of Cologne. This hilly landscape offers a range of hiking trails with varying difficulty levels. Hike through dense forests, open meadows, and quaint villages, experiencing the natural beauty of the German countryside.

6. **Eifel National Park:**

- *Description:* While a bit farther from Cologne, the Eifel National Park is a must-visit for nature enthusiasts. Discover extensive hiking trails that wind through unspoiled landscapes, dense forests, and picturesque lakes. The park's diverse ecosystems provide a rich tapestry for hikers to explore.

7. **Brühler Schlosspark (Brühl Palace Park):**

- *Description:* Just south of Cologne, the Brühler Schlosspark offers a delightful combination of history and nature. Explore the park's well-maintained paths, charming lakes, and historic structures. The serene atmosphere makes it an ideal location for a leisurely stroll or a relaxed day of exploration.

Whether you prefer a gentle walk along the Rhine or a more challenging trek through wooded hills, Cologne's hiking trails and trekking routes cater to a variety of preferences. Each trail promises a rejuvenating outdoor experience, allowing you to connect with nature just beyond the city limits in 2024.

Water Activities - Beaches, Snorkeling, and Diving

While Cologne may not be known for its coastal setting, the nearby rivers and lakes offer opportunities for water enthusiasts to engage in various aquatic activities. Dive into the refreshing water experiences available near the city:

1. **Rheinstrand Murmelbucht:**

   - *Description:* Located along the banks of the Rhine River, Rheinstrand Murmelbucht is a popular urban beach in Cologne. Relax on the sandy shores, soak up the sun, and enjoy the views of passing boats. The shallow waters make it an inviting spot for a refreshing dip on warm days.

2. **Agrippabad:**

   - *Description:* For those seeking a more structured aquatic experience, Agrippabad is a large indoor and outdoor swimming complex in Cologne. The outdoor pool area provides a pleasant space for swimming and sunbathing during the warmer months, offering a city-based aquatic retreat.

3. **Fühlinger See:**

   - *Description:* Fühlinger See is a large lake in the northern part of Cologne, offering not only serene waters but also a variety of water activities. Explore the lake by renting a paddleboat or canoe, or simply unwind on the lakeside beaches. The clear waters of Fühlinger See make it an excellent spot for a refreshing swim.

4. **Severinsbad:**

   - *Description:* Severinsbad is an historic bathhouse along the Rhine that combines tradition with modern amenities. The outdoor swimming pool area, with its panoramic views of the river, provides a unique setting for water activities. Enjoy a swim while taking in the cityscape and the river's gentle flow.

5. **Nordostbad:**

- *Description:* Nestled in the Cologne district of Mülheim, Nordostbad is a family-friendly swimming facility with outdoor pools for relaxation and aquatic fun. The spacious sunbathing areas and inviting waters make it an enjoyable destination for water enthusiasts of all ages.

6. **Ahr Valley:**

- *Description:* While not directly in Cologne, the Ahr Valley, a short drive south of the city, offers scenic river landscapes and opportunities for kayaking and canoeing.

7. **Diving Centers on the Rhine:**

- *Description:* Although not a traditional diving destination, some diving centers along the Rhine River offer opportunities for diving courses and experiences. While the visibility may not match tropical dive sites, exploring the underwater world of the Rhine can be a unique and adventurous experience.

While Cologne may not boast tropical beaches, its water-centric offerings provide a refreshing break from urban exploration. Whether lounging on the banks of the Rhine, enjoying the facilities of swimming complexes, or venturing to nearby lakes and rivers, water activities add an aquatic dimension to your Cologne adventure in 2024.

Adventure Sports and Outdoor Excursions
For thrill-seekers and outdoor enthusiasts, Cologne and its surrounding areas offer a plethora of exhilarating activities and adventurous excursions.

Dive into the world of adrenaline-pumping sports and outdoor exploration for an unforgettable experience:

1. **Hot Air Ballooning:**

   - *Description:* Soar above the picturesque landscapes surrounding Cologne with a hot air balloon ride. Experience the city and its outskirts from a unique vantage point as you glide through the sky. Several companies offer hot air balloon excursions, providing an opportunity for breathtaking views and a sense of adventure.

2. **Segway Tours:**

   - *Description:* Explore Cologne in a fun and innovative way by joining a Segway tour. Glide through the city's streets, parks, and riverside paths on these self-balancing vehicles. Guided tours offer a unique perspective of the city while adding an element of excitement to your sightseeing experience.

3. **Rock Climbing at CityRock Cologne:**

- *Description:* CityRock Cologne provides indoor rock climbing adventures for climbers of all skill levels. Whether you're a beginner or an experienced climber, the facility offers a variety of routes and challenges. It's an ideal place to test your climbing skills and enjoy a thrilling workout.

4. **Canopy Tours in Bergisch Gladbach:**

- *Description:* Just east of Cologne, in Bergisch Gladbach, you can embark on a canopy tour through the treetops. Experience the thrill of ziplining and navigating suspension bridges amidst the lush forest canopy. This outdoor adventure provides an exciting blend of adrenaline and natural beauty.

5. **Paragliding in the Eifel Region:**

- *Description:* Head to the Eifel region for an unforgettable paragliding experience.

Take to the skies and enjoy the sensation of free flight while soaking in breathtaking views of the Eifel landscape. Qualified instructors and tandem flights are available for both beginners and experienced paragliders.

6. **Bike Tours along the Rhine:**

  - *Description:* Embark on a cycling adventure along the scenic Rhine River. Explore the well-maintained bike paths that run parallel to the riverbanks, passing through charming villages, vineyards, and picturesque landscapes. Bike rentals are readily available in Cologne, providing an active and enjoyable way to discover the region.

7. **High Ropes Course at Kletterwald Neroberg:**

  - *Description:* Located a bit farther in Wiesbaden, Kletterwald Neroberg offers an exhilarating high ropes course adventure. Navigate through treetop obstacles and zip lines, testing your agility and nerve. The course caters to various skill levels, making it suitable for both beginners and seasoned adventurers.

8. **Stand-Up Paddleboarding (SUP) on the Rhine:**

- *Description:* Experience the tranquility of the Rhine River while engaging in the popular water sport of stand-up paddleboarding. Several operators in Cologne offer SUP rentals, allowing you to paddle along the river and enjoy a unique perspective of the city.

From flying high in a hot air balloon to navigating treetop obstacles, Cologne and its surroundings provide an array of adventure sports and outdoor excursions to satisfy every thrill-seeker's appetite.

Chapter 6: Immersing in Cologne Culture

Local Festivals and Events

Cologne is a city that knows how to celebrate, and its calendar is filled with vibrant festivals and events that showcase the rich cultural tapestry of the region. Immerse yourself in the lively atmosphere and join the locals in these festive occasions:

1. **Cologne Carnival (Kölner Karneval):**

   - *Description:* The Cologne Carnival is one of the most celebrated and iconic events in the city. Held in the weeks leading up to Lent, this lively festival is a spectacle of parades, colorful costumes, and exuberant street parties. Join the locals in shouting "Kölle Alaaf!" and immerse yourself in the infectious energy of the carnival.

2. **Rhine in Flames (Rhein in Flammen):**

   - *Description:* Experience the magic of Rhine in Flames, an annual event that transforms the banks of the Rhine River into a dazzling display of fireworks and light. Various locations along the river host this event throughout the summer, creating a breathtaking spectacle against the backdrop of Cologne's skyline.

3. **Christopher Street Day (CSD) Parade:**

- *Description:* Celebrate diversity and equality at the Christopher Street Day Parade, an annual event supporting the LGBTQ+ community. Join the colorful parade as it winds through the streets of Cologne, spreading messages of love, acceptance, and inclusion.

4. **Kölner Lichter (Cologne Lights):**

- *Description:* Kölner Lichter is an extraordinary event that illuminates the night sky with a spectacular fireworks display over the Rhine. Accompanied by music and a magical atmosphere, this event attracts crowds to the riverbanks for an enchanting evening.

5. **Gamescom:**

- *Description:* For gaming enthusiasts, Gamescom is a must-attend event. As one of the largest gaming conventions in the world, it gathers gamers, developers, and industry professionals. Explore the latest in gaming technology, attend workshops, and be part of the excitement at this international gaming extravaganza.

6. **Cologne Christmas Markets (Kölner Weihnachtsmärkte):**

- *Description:* Embrace the festive spirit during the Cologne Christmas Markets, where the city transforms into a winter wonderland. Multiple markets, each with its own theme and charm, offer a delightful array of crafts, seasonal treats, and holiday cheer. The aroma of mulled wine and the glow of twinkling lights create a magical atmosphere.

7. **Cologne Fine Art & Antiques Fair:**

- *Description:* Art enthusiasts will appreciate the Cologne Fine Art & Antiques Fair. Held annually, this event showcases a diverse collection of fine art, antiques, and decorative objects. Explore the exhibits from international galleries and discover unique pieces that span various artistic periods.

8. **Kölner Musiknacht (Cologne Music Night):**

- *Description:* Experience the city's vibrant music scene during Kölner Musiknacht, where numerous venues across Cologne come alive with live performances of various genres. From classical to contemporary, this musical extravaganza offers a night of entertainment for music lovers.

These festivals and events provide a glimpse into the dynamic cultural scene of Cologne. Whether you're drawn to the exuberance of the carnival, the enchantment of fireworks, or the artistic expressions at various fairs, immersing yourself in local festivities allows you to connect with the heart and soul of the city in 2024.

Traditional Music, Dance, and Art

Cologne's cultural heritage is deeply rooted in its traditional music, dance, and art, providing a captivating glimpse into the city's rich history and artistic expressions. Delve into the vibrant world of Cologne's cultural traditions:

1. **Kölner Philharmonie:**

   - *Description:* The Kölner Philharmonie stands as a symbol of Cologne's commitment to classical music. Attend a performance by the renowned Gürzenich Orchestra or international guest artists in this architectural masterpiece. The philharmonic hall's acoustics and design create a captivating space for classical music enthusiasts.

2. **Rheinische Musikschule (Rhenish Music School):**

   - *Description:* Immerse yourself in the world of music at the Rheinische Musikschule, where a diverse range of music classes, workshops, and concerts take place. The institution plays a vital role in nurturing musical talent and fostering a love for music among Cologne's residents.

3. **Hänneschen-Theater:**

   - *Description:* Experience the charm of puppetry at the Hänneschen-Theater, one of the oldest puppet theaters in Germany. The theater's resident characters, Hänneschen and Bärbelchen, have been entertaining audiences with traditional Cologne tales for generations.

Attend a performance to witness the magic of puppetry and local storytelling.

4. **Tanzbrunnen:**

- *Description:* The Tanzbrunnen, an open-air venue on the banks of the Rhine, hosts a variety of cultural events, including concerts, dance performances, and theater productions. Attend a live show under the open sky and enjoy the riverside ambiance that adds a special touch to the cultural experience.

5. **Cologne Opera (Oper Köln):**

- *Description:* Immerse yourself in the world of opera and ballet at the Cologne Opera. The impressive building hosts a repertoire ranging from classic operas to contemporary productions, showcasing the city's commitment to the performing arts.

6. **Cologne Cathedral Concerts (Kölner Dom Konzerte):**

   - *Description:* The Cologne Cathedral provides a breathtaking backdrop for classical concerts that resonate within its historic walls. Attend one of the cathedral concerts to experience the fusion of music and architectural grandeur, creating a truly memorable cultural experience.

7. **Museum Ludwig:**

   - *Description:* Museum Ludwig is a haven for modern and contemporary art lovers. Explore the extensive collection featuring works by iconic artists such as Picasso, Warhol, and Beuys. The museum's commitment to showcasing diverse artistic expressions makes it a must-visit for art enthusiasts.

8. **Ehrenfelder Schauspielhaus:**

- *Description:* The Ehrenfelder Schauspielhaus, located in the vibrant Ehrenfeld district, is a cultural hub that promotes local theater productions, dance performances, and art exhibitions. Attend a show to witness the creativity and innovation emanating from Cologne's artistic community.

9. **Cologne Carnival Songs:**

- *Description:* The Cologne Carnival is not only a visual spectacle but also a celebration of music. Dive into the lively atmosphere with traditional carnival songs, known as "Fastelovend" tunes. These cheerful and infectious melodies capture the spirit of the carnival season.

Cologne's commitment to preserving and celebrating its cultural heritage is evident in the variety of traditional music, dance, and art experiences available. Whether you choose to attend a classical concert, explore contemporary art, or immerse yourself in the local puppetry tradition, each cultural encounter contributes to the dynamic and diverse tapestry of Cologne's artistic landscape in 2024.

Interaction with Locals and Cultural Etiquette

Cologne's charm extends beyond its landmarks; it lies in the warmth and friendliness of its residents. To truly immerse yourself in the local culture, understanding the etiquette and fostering connections with the friendly locals is key:

**1. Greet with a Smile:

- **Etiquette:** Germans, including the people of Cologne, appreciate a friendly smile and a warm greeting. When entering shops, restaurants, or engaging with locals in various settings, don't hesitate to offer a genuine smile and a polite "Guten Tag" (Good day) or "Hallo."

**2. Respect Personal Space:

- **Etiquette:** Germans value personal space, and it's customary to maintain a respectful distance in public places. Avoid standing too close to others in queues or crowded areas. This practice ensures a comfortable and considerate environment for everyone.

**3. Use Formal Titles:

- **Etiquette:** When interacting with strangers or in formal settings, it's common to use formal titles like "Herr" (Mr.) or "Frau" (Mrs./Ms.) followed by the person's last name. This adds a touch of politeness and is appreciated in professional and unfamiliar situations.

**4. Kölsch Dialect and English Language:

- **Interaction:** While many locals speak Kölsch, the regional dialect, most are fluent in German and English. Attempting a few basic German phrases can be appreciated, but don't hesitate to switch to English if needed. The people of Cologne are generally welcoming to tourists and appreciate efforts to communicate.

5. Engage in Small Talk:

- **Interaction:** Germans, including the people of Cologne, engage in polite small talk. Casual conversations about the weather, local events, or cultural aspects can be a great way to connect. Don't be shy to initiate friendly discussions; it's a common practice.

6. Respect Local Customs and Traditions:

- **Etiquette:** Cologne has a strong cultural identity, and locals take pride in their traditions, especially during events like the Cologne Carnival. Respect local customs and be open to participating in festivities. Learning about and embracing the local culture fosters a sense of connection with the community.

7. Tipping Etiquette:

- **Etiquette:** Tipping is customary in restaurants and cafes. It's common to round up the bill or leave a tip of around 5-10%, depending on the service. In bars, it's usual to leave small change as a tip.

**8. Attend Local Events and Festivals:

- **Interaction:** Participating in local events and festivals provides excellent opportunities to engage with the community. Whether it's joining in the Cologne Carnival parades, attending concerts, or exploring the Christmas markets, these events offer a chance to connect with locals in a festive atmosphere.

**9. Cultural Sensitivity:

- **Etiquette:** Demonstrating cultural sensitivity is essential. Avoid sensitive topics in conversation, and be mindful of differences in customs and traditions. Showing respect for local customs fosters positive interactions and enhances your cultural experience.

Interacting with the people of Cologne is an integral part of your journey. Embrace the friendly atmosphere, respect local customs, and you'll find that engaging with the locals adds a layer of authenticity to your exploration of Cologne's rich cultural tapestry in 2024.

Chapter 7: Practical Tips for a Smooth Stay

Currency, Banking, and Communication

Navigating the practical aspects of currency, banking, and communication is crucial for a seamless and enjoyable stay in Cologne. Here's a guide to help you manage these essentials:

1. Currency:

- **Official Currency:** The official currency in Germany is the Euro (€). Ensure you have some cash on hand for small purchases, especially in areas where card payments may not be widely accepted.

- **ATMs:** ATMs (Automated Teller Machines) are prevalent in Cologne, allowing you to withdraw cash conveniently. They are commonly found at banks, train stations, and major shopping areas. Check with your bank regarding international withdrawal fees.

- **Currency Exchange:** Currency exchange services are available at banks, exchange offices, and airports. However, withdrawing cash from ATMs often provides a more favorable exchange rate.

2. Banking:

- **Bank Opening Hours:** Banks in Germany typically operate from Monday to Friday, with varying hours. Standard banking hours are from 9:00 AM to 4:00 PM, and some banks may close earlier on Fridays. ATMs are available 24/7 for cash withdrawal.

- **Credit and Debit Cards:** Credit and debit cards are widely accepted in Cologne, especially in restaurants, hotels, and larger shops. Visa and MasterCard are the most commonly used cards, but it's advisable to carry some cash for smaller establishments.

- **Bank Accounts:** If you plan to stay for an extended period, consider opening a local bank account for ease of transactions and potential cost savings on fees.

3. Communication:

- **Language:** German is the official language in Cologne. While many locals speak English, especially in tourist areas, learning a few basic German phrases can enhance your interactions and be appreciated by the locals.

- **Mobile Networks:** Cologne has excellent mobile network coverage. Ensure that your mobile phone is unlocked if you plan to use a local SIM card. Alternatively, check with your home provider regarding international roaming options.

- **Internet Connectivity:** Wi-Fi is widely available in hotels, cafes, and public spaces. If you need continuous internet access, consider purchasing a local SIM card or activating an international roaming plan.

- **Emergency Services:** The emergency number for police, medical assistance, and fire services in Germany is 112. Save this number in your contacts for quick access in case of emergencies.

4. Safety Precautions:

- **Secure Your Belongings:** Keep your belongings secure, especially in crowded places or public transport. Be cautious of pickpockets, and use anti-theft measures for your valuables.

- **Health Insurance:** Ensure you have comprehensive travel insurance that includes health coverage. The European Health Insurance Card (EHIC) may provide coverage for EU citizens, but non-EU citizens should have adequate travel insurance.

- **Local Laws and Customs:** Familiarize yourself with local laws and customs to ensure a respectful and lawful stay. For example, jaywalking is not allowed in Germany, and it's essential to follow traffic rules.

Understanding the practical aspects of currency, banking, and communication will contribute to a smooth and enjoyable stay in Cologne. Whether you're exploring the city's attractions, enjoying local cuisine, or participating in cultural events, these practical tips will enhance your overall travel experience in 2024.

Health and Safety Precautions

Prioritizing health and safety is paramount for a worry-free and enjoyable stay in Cologne. Follow these essential precautions to ensure your well-being throughout your visit:

1. Travel Insurance:

- **Recommendation:** Obtain comprehensive travel insurance that covers medical emergencies, trip cancellations, and other unforeseen events.

2. Vaccinations and Health Checks:

- **Routine Vaccinations:** Ensure your routine vaccinations are up-to-date. Check with your healthcare provider for recommended vaccinations for travel to Germany.

3. Medical Facilities:

- **Quality of Healthcare:** Cologne boasts a high standard of healthcare facilities. In case of medical concerns, seek assistance from reputable clinics, hospitals, or pharmacies.

- **Pharmacies:** Pharmacies (Apotheke) are widely available and can provide over-the-counter medications. Pharmacists often speak English and can offer advice on minor health issues.

4. Safety Precautions:

- **Personal Safety:** Cologne is generally a safe city, but exercise common sense precautions. Keep an eye on your belongings, avoid poorly lit areas at night, and use reputable transportation services.

- **Traffic Safety:** Follow traffic rules and be cautious when crossing streets. Use designated crosswalks and obey traffic signals to ensure your safety.

- **Emergency Services:** Familiarize yourself with the emergency number, 112, which covers police, medical assistance, and fire services. Be ready to provide clear information about your location in case of an emergency.

5. Hygiene Practices:

- **Hand Hygiene:** Maintain good hand hygiene by washing hands regularly with soap and water. Carry hand sanitizer for situations where washing facilities are not readily available.

- **Respiratory Etiquette:** Follow respiratory etiquette by covering your mouth and nose with a tissue or your elbow when coughing or sneezing. Dispose of tissues appropriately and avoid touching your face.

6. Local Laws and Customs:

- **Legal Considerations:** Familiarize yourself with local laws and customs to avoid unintentional legal issues. For example, public drinking is regulated in certain areas, and smoking may be restricted.

- **Cultural Sensitivity:** Respect cultural norms and be aware of potential sensitivities. Be considerate of local customs, especially in religious or historical sites.

By prioritizing health and safety precautions, you contribute to a secure and enjoyable experience in Cologne. Stay informed, follow guidelines, and take necessary measures to safeguard your well-being throughout your journey in 2024.

Language Basics - Useful Phrases for Travelers

While many people in Cologne speak English, making an effort to use a few basic German phrases can enhance your travel experience and create positive interactions. Here are some essential phrases to help you navigate daily situations:

1. Greetings and Politeness:

- *Hello:* Guten Tag (Goot-en tahk)

- *Goodbye:* Auf Wiedersehen (Owf Vee-der-zay-en)

- *Please:* Bitte (Bee-teh)

- *Thank you:* Danke (Dahn-kuh)

- *Excuse me / Sorry:* Entschuldigung (Ent-shool-dee-gung)

2. Basic Communication:

- *Yes:* Ja (Yah)

- *No:* Nein (Nine)

- *I don't understand:* Ich verstehe nicht (Ikh fer-shtay-uh nikht)

- *Do you speak English?:* Sprechen Sie Englisch? (Shpre-khen zee Eng-lish?)

3. Asking for Help:

- *Help:* Hilfe (Hil-feh)

- *Where is...?:* Wo ist...? (Voh ist...?)

- *I need a doctor:* Ich brauche einen Arzt (Ikh brow-khe eye-nen ahrtz)

4. Ordering Food and Drinks:

- *Menu, please:* Die Speisekarte, bitte (Dee shpy-suh-kar-tuh, bee-teh)

- *Water:* Wasser (Vah-ser)

- *Coffee:* Kaffee (Kah-fay)

- *Beer:* Bier (Beer)

- *The check, please:* Die Rechnung, bitte (Dee rek-noonk, bee-teh)

5. Transportation:

- *Train station:* Bahnhof (Bahnhof)

- *Bus stop:* Bushaltestelle (Boos-hahl-teh-shtel-leh)

- *Taxi:* Taxi (Tak-see)

- *How much is the fare?:* Wie viel kostet die Fahrt? (Vee feel kohstet dee fahrt?)

6. Shopping:

- *How much does this cost?:* Wie viel kostet das? (Vee feel kohstet dahs?)

- *I would like to buy...:* Ich möchte... (Ikh murkhte...)

- *Can I pay with a credit card?:* Kann ich mit Kreditkarte bezahlen? (Kahn ikh mit kray-deet-kar-te bezah-len?)

7. Emergencies:

- *Emergency:* Notfall (Nohht-fahl)

- *Police:* Polizei (Poh-lee-tsey)

- *Hospital:* Krankenhaus (Krahnk-en-haus)

- *I need help:* Ich brauche Hilfe (Ikh brow-khe hil-feh)

8. Expressing Gratitude:

- *You're welcome:* Bitte schön (Bee-teh shern)

- *Thank you very much:* Vielen Dank (Fee-len dahnk)

- *It was a pleasure:* Es war mir ein Vergnügen (Es var meer eye-n fer-kneh-gen)

Using these phrases demonstrates your respect for the local culture and will likely be met with appreciation. Even if your German is limited, locals generally appreciate the effort to communicate in their language.

Chapter 8: Cologne Souvenirs and Shopping

Unique Local Products and Handicrafts

Cologne offers a diverse range of unique local products and handicrafts that make for perfect souvenirs or gifts. Immerse yourself in the city's vibrant shopping scene and explore these distinctive items:

1. Eau de Cologne:

- *Description:* The world-famous "Eau de Cologne" originated in Cologne in the 18th century. This light and citrusy fragrance, often associated with the brand 4711, is a quintessential Cologne souvenir. Pick up a bottle to capture the essence of the city.

2. Kölsch Beer Glasses:

- *Description:* Kölsch is more than just a beer; it's a cultural experience in Cologne. Bring home the spirit of the local brew by purchasing traditional Kölsch beer glasses. These slender glasses are designed specifically for serving

Kölsch and are often adorned with the logos of different breweries.

3. Cologne Cathedral Souvenirs:

- *Description:* The Cologne Cathedral, a UNESCO World Heritage Site, is an iconic symbol of the city. You'll find an array of souvenirs featuring the cathedral, including miniature replicas, postcards, and artwork. These items beautifully capture the architectural grandeur of this historic landmark.

4. Printen (Gingerbread):

- *Description:* Indulge your taste buds with Printen, a type of spiced gingerbread cookie that has deep roots in Cologne. These sweet treats come in various flavors and shapes, making them a delightful and delicious souvenir to share with friends and family.

5. Zündorfer Original Reissdorf Kölsch Soap:

- *Description:* Uniquely crafted, Zündorfer Original Reissdorf Kölsch soap captures the essence of Cologne's most famous beer. Made with the actual beer, this soap not only cleans but also leaves you with a subtle hint of the city's beloved brew.

6. Cologne Stollen:

- *Description:* Stollen, a traditional German Christmas cake, is a delightful delicacy associated with the holiday season. Loaded with dried fruits, nuts, and spices, Cologne's version of Stollen is a perfect edible souvenir to enjoy or share during festive occasions.

7. Cologne Skyline Artwork:

- *Description:* Bring a piece of Cologne's skyline into your home with artwork depicting the city's landmarks. From paintings and prints to photographs, local artists capture the beauty of Cologne's architecture and landscapes in unique and captivating ways.

8. Handcrafted Kuckuck (Cuckoo) Clocks:

- *Description:* For a charming and functional souvenir, consider a handcrafted Kuckuck clock. Originating from the Black Forest region but widely available in Cologne, these traditional cuckoo clocks add a touch of German craftsmanship to your home.

9. Lindt Chocolate:

- *Description:* While Lindt is a Swiss brand, the Lindt Chocolate Museum in Cologne offers exclusive chocolate creations inspired by the city. Indulge in unique chocolate varieties that blend Swiss expertise with Cologne's sweet touch.

10. Local Artisan Crafts:

- *Description:* Explore Cologne's markets and artisan shops for handmade crafts by local artists. From pottery and jewelry to textiles and leather goods, these unique pieces reflect the creativity and craftsmanship of the Cologne community.

Venture into the city's markets, boutique stores, specialty shops to discover these unique products and handicrafts. Whether you're taking home a fragrant memory, a piece of Cologne's culinary heritage, or a beautifully crafted souvenir, these items serve as tangible reminders of your unforgettable journey in 2024.

Best Markets and Shopping Districts

Cologne boasts a vibrant shopping scene, offering a mix of modern shopping districts and traditional markets. Dive into the city's diverse retail landscape, and explore the best markets and shopping districts for a delightful shopping experience:

1. Cologne Cathedral and Surrounding Area:

- *Description:* The area around the Cologne Cathedral is a shopping haven, featuring both renowned international brands and local boutiques. From high-end fashion to unique souvenir shops, this central location offers a diverse range of shopping opportunities.

2. Ehrenstraße:

- *Description:* Ehrenstraße, located in the Belgian Quarter (Belgisches Viertel), is a trendy street known for its fashionable boutiques, concept stores, and independent shops. It's the perfect spot for those seeking eclectic fashion, accessories, and unique lifestyle items.

3. Schildergasse:

- *Description:* Schildergasse, one of the busiest shopping streets in Europe, is home to an array of department stores, flagship stores, and international brands. This bustling street provides a modern shopping experience and is ideal for fashion enthusiasts.

4. Neumarkt Galerie:

- *Description:* Neumarkt Galerie is a contemporary shopping mall offering a mix of fashion, beauty, and lifestyle stores. With its central location, it provides a convenient and diverse shopping experience.

5. Neustadt-Nord:

- *Description:* Neustadt-Nord is a neighborhood with a bohemian vibe and a rich selection of independent shops and vintage stores. Explore the narrow streets to discover hidden gems, unique clothing, and one-of-a-kind items crafted by local artisans.

6. Cologne Christmas Markets:

- *Description:* During the festive season, Cologne transforms into a winter wonderland with its famous Christmas markets. The markets, such as the ones at Cologne Cathedral and Alter Markt, offer a magical atmosphere with twinkling lights and stalls selling handcrafted ornaments, festive treats, and local crafts.

7. Lindenthal:

- *Description:* Lindenthal, a charming district with a mix of historic and modern elements, provides a unique shopping experience. Explore local shops offering artisanal products, antiques, and specialty items in this picturesque neighborhood.

8. Agnesviertel:

- *Description:* Agnesviertel is known for its artistic and alternative atmosphere. The district is home to a variety of independent stores, galleries, and vintage shops. It's a great place to find quirky and distinctive items that reflect the local culture.

9. Wochenmarkt am Kölner Rudolfplatz (Rudolfplatz Weekly Market):

- *Description:* For a taste of local flavors, visit the weekly market at Rudolfplatz. This market offers fresh produce, regional specialties, and handmade products. It's an excellent opportunity to engage with local vendors and experience the city's culinary scene.

10. Hohenzollernring:

- *Description:* Hohenzollernring, encircling the city center, is a lively street with a mix of shops, cafes, and bars. This area is particularly popular for its vibrant nightlife, and during the day, it offers a range of boutique stores and unique finds.

Cologne's markets and shopping districts cater to a diverse range of tastes and preferences. Whether you're seeking luxury brands, local craftsmanship, or the charm of traditional markets, the city provides a dynamic and rewarding shopping experience in 2024.

Chapter 9: Accommodation Guide

Types of accommodations available

Cologne offers a diverse range of accommodations to suit every traveler's preferences and budget. From luxury hotels to charming guesthouses, the city provides a variety of options for a comfortable stay. Explore the types of accommodations available in Cologne:

1. Luxury Hotels:

- *Description:* Cologne boasts a selection of upscale hotels, often located in prime city center locations or along the scenic Rhine River. These luxury accommodations offer lavish amenities, spacious rooms, fine dining, and personalized services for those seeking a premium experience.

2. Boutique Hotels:

- *Description:* Boutique hotels in Cologne combine unique design elements with personalized service. These smaller, stylish accommodations often showcase distinctive themes or historical charm, providing an intimate and immersive stay.

3. Business Hotels:

- *Description:* Catering to corporate travelers, business hotels in Cologne offer amenities such as conference facilities, meeting rooms, high-speed internet, and convenient access to business districts. These accommodations ensure a seamless stay for those traveling for work.

4. Budget and Mid-Range Hotels:

- *Description:* Cologne provides a range of budget-friendly and mid-range hotels suitable for travelers seeking comfort without breaking the bank. These accommodations offer essential amenities, clean and well-appointed rooms, and convenient locations throughout the city.

5. Vacation Rentals and Apartments:

- *Description:* For a more independent stay, vacation rentals and apartments are available in various neighborhoods. These options provide the flexibility of self-catering and a home-like atmosphere, ideal for those looking to experience Cologne like a local.

6. Hostels:

- *Description:* Hostels offer budget-friendly accommodation with shared dormitories or private rooms. Ideal for solo travelers, backpackers, or those looking for a social atmosphere, hostels often provide communal spaces, organized activities, and a diverse mix of international guests.

7. Guesthouses and Bed and Breakfasts:

- *Description:* Guesthouses and bed and breakfasts in Cologne offer a more personalized and intimate lodging experience. Typically run by local hosts, these accommodations provide cozy rooms and homemade breakfasts, creating a warm and welcoming environment.

8. Serviced Apartments:

- *Description:* Serviced apartments provide a blend of hotel-style services and the independence of an apartment. Equipped with kitchens or kitchenettes, these accommodations are suitable for extended stays, offering a homey atmosphere with the convenience of hotel amenities.

9. Wellness and Spa Hotels:

- *Description:* Wellness and spa hotels in Cologne focus on providing relaxation and rejuvenation. With on-site spa facilities, wellness programs, and tranquil surroundings, these accommodations are perfect for travelers seeking a soothing and wellness-oriented stay.

10. Unique Accommodations:

- *Description:* For a truly distinctive experience, Cologne offers unique accommodations such as houseboats on the Rhine, historic castle stays, and themed accommodations. These options add an extra layer of novelty and charm to your visit.

When selecting accommodation in Cologne, consider your preferences, travel purpose, and budget. The city's diverse range of lodging options ensures that every traveler can find a suitable and comfortable place to stay while exploring the vibrant attractions and cultural richness of Cologne in 2024.

Recommendations for Various Budgets and Preferences

Cologne caters to a wide range of budgets and preferences when it comes to accommodation. Whether you're looking for luxury, a cozy bed and breakfast, or a budget-friendly stay, here are some recommendations to guide you based on your preferences:

1. Luxury Retreats:

- *Recommendation:* For an indulgent stay, consider the Excelsior Hotel Ernst, a 5-star luxury hotel located near the Cologne Cathedral. With opulent rooms, gourmet dining, and a spa offering panoramic views of the city, it provides an exquisite experience.

2. Boutique Elegance:

- *Recommendation:* Immerse yourself in boutique elegance at the Hotel Im Wasserturm, a unique hotel set within a historic water tower. Located in the trendy Belgisches Viertel, this boutique gem offers stylish rooms and a blend of modern design with historic charm.

3. Budget-Friendly Comfort:

- *Recommendation:* Opt for the Ibis Köln Centrum for a budget-friendly yet comfortable stay. Centrally located, this hotel offers clean and modern rooms with essential amenities, making it an excellent choice for cost-conscious travelers.

4. Authentic Bed and Breakfast:

- *Recommendation:* Experience authentic Cologne hospitality at the Bed & Breakfast Cologne, a charming guesthouse in the heart of the city. With personalized service and cozy rooms, it provides a home-away-from-home atmosphere.

5. Urban Chic:

- *Recommendation:* Stay in urban chic surroundings at the 25hours Hotel The Circle. Located in the Friesenviertel district, this trendy hotel boasts unique design elements, a rooftop terrace, and vibrant communal spaces for a modern and stylish stay.

6. Backpacker's Haven:

- *Recommendation:* If you're a budget-conscious traveler, the Pathpoint Cologne Backpacker Hostel offers affordable dormitory-style accommodations with a social atmosphere. It's ideal for backpackers seeking a central location and a lively environment.

7. Apartment Living:

- *Recommendation:* Enjoy the flexibility of apartment living at the Maria Suite Apartments. These fully equipped apartments, located in the Agnesviertel district, provide a homey atmosphere with the convenience of a hotel.

8. Tranquil Wellness Retreat:

- *Recommendation:* Indulge in a tranquil wellness retreat at the Mauritius Hotel & Therme. This accommodation in the picturesque district of Bad Godesberg features thermal baths and a spa, offering a peaceful escape from the city hustle.

9. Quirky and Unique Stay:

- *Recommendation:* For a quirky and unique experience, book a stay at the Bootshaus Wiking, a houseboat located on the Rhine River. Wake up to scenic views and enjoy the novelty of staying on the water.

10. Family-Friendly Comfort:

- *Recommendation:* Families can find comfort at the Hyatt Regency Cologne, a family-friendly hotel with spacious rooms and amenities for children. Its central location and family-focused services make it an excellent choice for those traveling with kids.

Consider these recommendations based on your preferences and budget to ensure a comfortable and enjoyable stay in Cologne. With a variety of accommodations to choose from, you can tailor your lodging experience to match the unique charm and offerings of the city in 2024.

Conclusion

As your journey through the vibrant city of Cologne unfolds, we hope this comprehensive travel guide has been a valuable companion, offering insights and recommendations to enhance every aspect of your visit. Cologne, with its rich history, cultural treasures, and welcoming atmosphere, promises an unforgettable experience for every traveler.

From the majestic Cologne Cathedral dominating the skyline to the lively markets, diverse neighborhoods, and the warmth of its people, the city reveals a tapestry of experiences waiting to be explored. As you wander through the historic streets, indulge in culinary delights, and immerse yourself in the local culture, Cologne unveils its unique blend of tradition and modernity.

Whether you're captivated by the iconic landmarks, enchanted by the aroma of Eau de Cologne, or savoring the flavors of local cuisine, each moment in Cologne contributes to a tapestry of memories. Venture into hidden gems, embrace outdoor adventures, and participate in cultural celebrations to truly grasp the essence of this remarkable city.

Practical tips for a smooth stay, diverse accommodation options, and a spectrum of activities cater to every budget and preference, ensuring that your stay in Cologne is not just a visit but a personalized and enriching experience.

As you bid farewell to Cologne, we hope the memories woven during your stay linger as a testament to the city's charm and hospitality. May the echoes of laughter from local festivals, the taste of Cologne's culinary delights, and the beauty of its landmarks linger in your heart, inspiring you to return and explore even more facets of this enchanting city.

Cologne beckons with open arms, inviting you to become a part of its story, to weave your own adventures into the fabric of its history. Until we meet again in the heart of this welcoming city, may your travels be filled with discovery, joy, and the enduring spirit of Cologne.

Appendix

Maps and Navigational Tools

Navigating the charming streets and diverse neighborhoods of Cologne is made easier with the aid of modern maps and navigational tools. Whether you're exploring historical landmarks, finding hidden gems, or simply getting from one point to another, these resources will enhance your journey:

1. Google Maps:

- *Website:* www.google.com/maps

- **Description:** Google Maps is a comprehensive mapping tool that offers detailed maps, real-time navigation, and street views. It covers public transportation options, walking routes, and driving directions, making it an invaluable resource for exploring Cologne.

2. Cologne Official Tourist Map:

- *Website:* www.cologne-tourism.com/map

- **Description:** The official tourist map provided by the Cologne Tourist Board is a detailed guide to the city's attractions, public transportation routes, and key points of interest. It offers both online and downloadable versions for your convenience.

3. BVG Fahrinfo Plus (Public Transport App):

- *Website:* www.bvg.de/en

- **Description:** For efficient use of public transportation, the BVG Fahrinfo Plus app provides real-time schedules, route planning, and service updates. While originally designed for Berlin, it is a useful tool for navigating public transport in Cologne.

4. Komoot - Hiking and Biking Trails:

- *Website:* www.komoot.com

- **Description:** If you plan to explore Cologne's scenic outdoor trails, Komoot is an excellent app for hiking and biking enthusiasts. It offers detailed route planning, maps, and highlights points of interest along the way.

5. DB Navigator - Train Travel App:

- *Website:* www.bahn.com/en/view/index.shtml

- **Description:** The DB Navigator app by Deutsche Bahn is a valuable tool for navigating Germany's extensive train network. It provides real-time schedules, ticket booking, and platform information for train travel within and around Cologne.

6. HERE WeGo - Offline Maps and Navigation:

- *Website:* www.here.com

- **Description:** HERE WeGo offers offline maps and navigation, making it a useful tool for travelers without constant internet access. Download the maps of Cologne in advance and navigate the city seamlessly.

7. Cologne Bike City App:

- *Website:* www.koelner-fahrrad.de

- **Description:** For those exploring Cologne on two wheels, the Cologne Bike City app provides information on bike paths, rental stations, and cycling routes, enhancing your biking experience in the city.

8. Cologne Airport - Interactive Terminal Map:

- *Website:* www.cologne-bonn-airport.com/en

- **Description:** Navigating an airport can be a challenge, especially in a new city. The interactive terminal map on the Cologne Bonn Airport website helps you find your way around the airport efficiently.

Before embarking on your Cologne adventure, consider utilizing these maps and navigational tools to plan your routes, discover local attractions, and ensure a smooth and enjoyable exploration of the city. Whether you prefer digital apps or printed maps, these resources will be invaluable additions to your travel toolkit.